DELAWARE

The First State

Derek Miller, David King,
Brian Fitzgerald, and Kerry Jones Waring

Cavendish
Square

New York

Published in 2020 by Cavendish Square Publishing, LLC
243 5th Avenue, Suite 136, New York, NY 10016

Library of Congress Cataloging-in-Publication Data

Names: Miller, Derek L., author. | King, David C., author. |
FitzgeraldBrian, 1972- author. | Waring, Kerry Jones, author.
Title: Delaware / Derek Miller, David King, Brian Fitzgerald, and Kerry Jones Waring.
Description: Fourth edition. | New York : Cavendish Square, [2020] |
Series: It's my state! | Includes bibliographical references and index.
Identifiers: LCCN 2018033910 (print) | LCCN 2018034097 (ebook) |
ISBN 9781502641793 (ebook) | ISBN 9781502641786 (library bound) |
ISBN 9781502644473 (pbk.)
Subjects: LCSH: Delaware--Juvenile literature.
Classification: LCC F164.3 (ebook) | LCC F164.3 .K56 2020 (print) |
DDC 975.1--dc23
LC record available at https://lccn.loc.gov/2018033910

Editorial Director: David McNamara
Editor: Caitlyn Miller
Copy Editor: Nathan Heidelberger
Associate Art Director: Alan Sliwinski
Designer: Jessica Nevins
Production Coordinator: Karol Szymczuk
Photo Research: J8 Media

Printed in the United States of America

It's My STATE!

Table of Contents

SNAPSHOT
DELAWARE

Statehood

December 7, 1787

Population

961,939 (2017 census estimate)

Capital

Dover

State Flag

The background of Delaware's flag is colonial blue. In the center lies a buff-colored diamond. (Buff is a yellow-brown color.) The state coat of arms, which contains the same elements as the seal, lies in this diamond. Below the diamond, the words "December 7, 1787" appear. This is the date that Delaware ratified the US Constitution.

State Seal

The outer edge of Delaware's seal bears the words "Great Seal of the State of Delaware," and the years 1704, 1776, and 1787. These are the years that Delaware established its General Assembly, the Declaration of Independence was signed, and Delaware signed the US Constitution. In the middle of the seal are a farmer and militiaman flanking a sheaf of wheat, an ear of corn, and an ox. These images represent the central role of agriculture in the state, as well as the importance of citizen militias in defending liberty. The state motto, "Liberty and Independence," also appears on a banner.

HISTORICAL EVENTS TIMELINE

1609

The first European to sail into the Delaware Bay, Henry Hudson, claims the region for the Netherlands.

1638

Swedish colonists arrive in Delaware and found the colony of New Sweden, coming into conflict with the Dutch.

1664

The English conquer Delaware as we know it today, and the land is soon claimed by the colonies of Pennsylvania and Maryland.

State Song

Since 1925, the state song has been "Our Delaware." The words of the first three stanzas are from a 1906 George B. Hynson poem praising the state. Each of the first three stanzas corresponds to one of the three counties of Delaware. A fourth stanza and musical score were later additions to create the modern state song.

State Tree

The American holly is the state tree of Delaware. It is a very common and important tree in the state's forests. The holly is notable for its prickly foliage and bright red berries. The tree is also known as the Christmas holly due to its association with the holiday season.

State Flower

The peach blossom was adopted as the state flower in 1953, although it was first adopted as the state's floral emblem in 1895. This selection was based on the key role that peaches played in Delaware's early agriculture. The peach blossom itself is a light pink flower that is known for its beauty.

1776

The state of Delaware declares independence from Pennsylvania.

1777

Dover becomes Delaware's capital.

1787

Delaware becomes the first state to ratify the US Constitution.

Delaware Blue Hen

1964

The Cape May-Lewes Ferry makes its first trip.

1971

Delaware's government displays its concern for the environment with the passage of the Coastal Zone Act, which forbids heavy industry from operating near the coast.

1981

The Financial Center Development Act is signed into law in Delaware, bringing major banks to the state. Many are still headquartered in Delaware today.

Belemnite

The state fossil came from sea creatures that are now extinct but are believed to be related to squid.

State Bug

Ladybug

CURRENT EVENTS TIMELINE

2000

The first female governor of Delaware, Ruth Ann Minner, is elected.

2009

Former Delaware senator Joe Biden is sworn in as the vice president of the United States.

2017

A rare earthquake rocks the East Coast. Its epicenter is in Delaware.

Rehoboth Beach features sun, sand, and history. Shown here is one of eleven triangulation towers that date to World War II.

1 Geography

Delaware lies on the East Coast, nestled between Maryland, Pennsylvania, and New Jersey. This strategically important location led Thomas Jefferson to call it a "jewel"— and one of its unofficial nicknames is "The Diamond State" as a result. The fascinating history of Delaware is tied to its location. Delaware is tightly linked to the rest of the East Coast, and throughout American history people have been drawn to the First State.

Counties and Regions

Delaware is just 96 miles (155 kilometers) long, and it is very narrow. The state is only 35 miles (56 km) across at its widest point. Delaware has only three counties, the fewest of any state. More than half of the people live in the northern county of New Castle. Wilmington, the largest city in Delaware, is in New Castle County. Kent County in central Delaware is home to Dover, the state capital. Kent and the southernmost county of Sussex are more rural and less heavily populated.

FAST FACT

Delaware's official state nickname is "The First State" because it was the first to ratify the US Constitution on December 7, 1787. Other states were not so quick to approve the document. The last state to ratify the Constitution, Rhode Island, did so in May 1790.

Delaware borders Pennsylvania and Maryland. New Jersey is across the Delaware River and Delaware Bay.

Most of Delaware sits on a long **peninsula**—a stretch of land that is surrounded by water on three sides. This area, called the Delmarva Peninsula, also includes parts of Maryland and Virginia. The peninsula's name is a combination of the names of those three states. The Delaware River, Delaware Bay, and the Atlantic Ocean border the eastern side of the peninsula. The Chesapeake Bay lies on its western side.

Delaware has only two geographic regions. Most of the state is part of the Atlantic Coastal Plain—a narrow belt of lowland that extends from New York to Florida. Delaware is the lowest state in the country. The average elevation is just 60 feet (18 meters) above sea level.

A narrow strip of land in northern Delaware is part of a region called the Piedmont. This area of gently rolling hills lies between the Atlantic Coastal Plain and the Appalachian Mountains. Delaware's highest point is found in this area, very close to the Pennsylvania border. A spot near Ebright Road in New Castle County rises 448 feet (137 m) above sea level. Delaware's highest point is much lower than the lowest point in many other states.

The marshy land in the southern part of the state forms the famous Great Cypress Swamp. The 30,000-acre (12,140-hectare) swamp is also known as the Great Pocomoke Swamp.

Delaware's Waterways

Delaware has 381 miles (613 km) of shoreline—a surprising amount for such a small state. Much of the coast borders Delaware Bay. This area has many shallow coves, sandy beaches, and marshy areas.

The Great Cypress Swamp is shared by Delaware and Maryland.

Delaware meets the Atlantic Ocean on the eastern edge of Sussex County. The sandy ocean coastline stretches 28 miles (45 km), from the Maryland border in the south to Cape Henlopen at the mouth of Delaware Bay. Rehoboth Beach and Bethany Beach are two of Delaware's most popular tourist destinations. A large part of this coastal area is a low sandbar that separates the ocean from the Rehoboth and Indian River bays.

Cape Henlopen is home to Cape Henlopen State Park.

Many small islands dot the coastline. The largest are Pea Patch Island and Reedy Island in the Delaware River. Pea Patch Island is home to Fort Delaware State Park. During the Civil War (1861–1865), the fort was used as a prison. Fenwick Island is near the state's southern border. It is a busy vacation spot during the summer.

A low sandy ridge extends north and south through the state just inside Delaware's western border. This ridge is the edge of one of the state's watersheds (land areas draining into bodies of water). The state's rivers flow either east into the Delaware River or Delaware Bay, or west into Chesapeake Bay. The Delaware River starts in New York State and flows south for more than 300 miles (483 km) before emptying into Delaware Bay. The river is one of the key shipping routes on the East Coast. A human-made waterway—the Chesapeake and Delaware Canal—cuts across the state just south

Bethany Beach is one of Delaware's top tourist attractions.

Fenwick Island boasts beach favorites like a lighthouse, mini golf, and a boardwalk.

The Delaware River and Delaware Bay connect Delaware with major cities on the East Coast.

NEW YORK

NEW JERSEY

PENNSYLVANIA

MARYLAND

New York City

Trenton

Philadelphia

Camden

Wilmington

Reading

Baltimore

Dover

Washington

Atlantic Ocean

DELAWARE

About 200 miles (322 km) across

Delaware is a great place to enjoy fall colors.

of Wilmington. The canal connects Delaware Bay and Chesapeake Bay. These waterways played a vital role in Delaware's economic development by linking the state with major cities, especially Philadelphia and Baltimore.

Climate

Delaware has a moderate climate. Summers in most of the state are humid, with temperatures averaging between 70 and 80 degrees Fahrenheit (21 to 27 degrees Celsius). Ocean breezes make coastal areas a little cooler than the rest of the state. As summer turns to fall, leaves on trees begin to change colors. Residents and visitors alike enjoy the cooler weather and vivid colors of fall.

Winters in the First State are not as harsh as winters in more northern states. The mountainous regions of Pennsylvania block cold northwestern winds from hitting Delaware. The average winter temperature is about 36°F (2°C). Warm ocean currents keep coastal areas warmer than inland areas. The amount of snowfall varies from the north to the south. Wilmington gets about 20 inches (51 centimeters) of snow each year. Towns in Sussex County often get far less.

Hagley Museum and Library and Other Top Attractions

One of Delaware's major tourist attractions celebrates the state's association with the du Pont family. The Hagley Museum and Library stretches across 235 acres (95 ha) in Wilmington. It encompasses the old gunpowder mill where E. I. du Pont started the family business. On the grounds of the museum, visitors can learn about how gunpowder was produced in early America. The lives of the workers at the old mill are also explored. Exhibits trace the history of the du Pont family and company. They examine the fascinating example of American entrepreneurship that took place on these grounds and continues to this day in Delaware.

The Hagley Museum and Library celebrates the achievements of the du Pont family.

Delaware's scenic coastline also draws tourists to the state. Visitors often stay in towns like Rehoboth Beach, Lewes Beach, and Fenwick Island. From there, they can enjoy the sun and sand and explore the surrounding area.

Beautiful natural areas like Cape Henlopen State Park and Bombay Hook National Wildlife Refuge are a short drive away. Visitors tired of the bustling beach towns can relax surrounded by nature. Pristine beaches and opportunities for bird-watching blanket these protected areas. No matter what you are looking for in a beach vacation, Delaware likely has it!

It's easy to enjoy Delaware's forests on the state's many trails.

Wildlife

About 30 percent of Delaware is covered by forests. Delaware and the whole Delmarva Peninsula are in a zone that includes both northern and southern plant life. Trees common to northern states are abundant, including oak, maple, hickory, and poplar. Trees that are found mainly in southern states, such as bald cypress, sweet gum, and loblolly pine, also thrive in Delaware.

From March to October, Delaware's level fields and meadows seem to be carpeted in wildflowers. The display begins in late winter with the first blossoming of crocuses and violets and extends through the asters and mums of late autumn. A number of flowering plants grow throughout spring and summer, including azaleas, morning glories, trumpet vines, and butterfly weeds. Water lilies and floating hearts add color to the many ponds, while pink and white hibiscus dot the marshy areas. Some swampland is almost impassable because of the thickets of wild blueberry and cranberry.

Delaware also has an abundance of wildlife. Its largest common wild animal is deer, although occasionally a black bear strays into the northern reaches of the state. Others include rabbits, minks, otters, both red and gray foxes, muskrats, and raccoons. Diamondback terrapins live in marshy areas near the coast, and snapping turtles are common in and around swamps. Amphibians such as frogs, toads, and salamanders also live in the damp areas around water or on wet forest floors. You are never far from water in Delaware—whether it's the ocean,

Bombay Hook National Wildlife Refuge

Delaware Bay, the many rivers and streams, or the state's fifty small lakes and ponds.

Bird-watching is a favorite pastime for many in Delaware. More than 275 bird species have been identified within Bombay Hook National Wildlife Refuge on the shore of Delaware Bay. This amazing number includes songbirds such as blue jays, robins, and cardinals. Shorebirds such as herons and egrets, and a variety of ducks can also be found on its marshy shores. Each spring, the 16,000-acre (6,475 ha) refuge is a stopping point for migrating shorebirds. Up to one million birds feed along the shores of the bay before continuing their journey north. Similarly, the dunes of Fenwick Island State Park are popular for observing black skimmers, osprey, and piping plovers.

The state's many sources of freshwater, along with the salt water of Delaware Bay and the Atlantic Ocean, provide a great variety of fish. Many people enjoy surf fishing on the Atlantic beaches or taking chartered boats to search for flounder, rockfish, and weakfish. Closer to shore, the coastal waters provide shad and striped bass. Clamming and crabbing are also popular around Delaware Bay. Freshwater fish in rivers and ponds include bluegill, perch, and catfish.

Fighting Pollution

Lawmakers in Delaware have taken steps to preserve the state's environment and natural resources. By the 1970s, the growth of Delaware's cities and suburbs and the increase in factories and motor vehicles were filling the air with a yellowish haze. In the waterways, the harvest of fish and shellfish dropped off so sharply that many commercial fishers were forced out of the trade.

Piping plovers are known to make a home in Fenwick Island State Park.

A family goes clamming together in the Indian River Inlet.

FAST FACT

Delaware's location on the East Coast is a major factor in the state's growth and economy. It is within 125 miles (200 km) of New York City; Washington, DC; Baltimore; and Philadelphia. This makes Delaware an attractive place to live and run a business.

What Lives in Delaware?

Flora

Bald Cypress *Taxodium distichum* is a large tree that grows in swampy areas. It is notable for its "knees." These are growths that jut out of the ground from the tree's roots. Their exact purpose is a mystery. Delaware's Great Cypress Swamp is the northernmost point in the United States where these southern trees thrive.

Coast Azalea *Rhododendron atlanticum* is a common shrub found in forests and gardens across Delaware and the East Coast. Coast azaleas grow in the shade of trees and are recognizable from their strong, fragrant scent. In the spring, they bloom and are covered with white, sometimes pinkish, flowers.

Dogwood *Cornus florida* is a small tree, rarely reaching 40 feet (12 m) in height. It is native to Delaware and commonly planted there for its beautiful appearance. Dogwoods have special white leaves, called bracts, that look like white flower blossoms. The dogwood's flower is actually in the center of the four bracts. In the fall, dogwoods are covered with small red berries that attract birds.

Sweet Goldenrod *Solidago odora* is a wildflower that flourishes in Delaware. It has many small, yellow flowers that smell like licorice. It is Delaware's state herb because its leaves can be used to make tea.

Sycamore *Platanus occidentalis* is a massive tree with the largest trunk of any tree in the eastern United States. It can grow up to 150 feet (46 m) tall, and its trunk can sometimes reach 16 feet (5 m) in diameter! It is often selected as a decorative plant because it is so fast-growing. Its wood is hard and used for many purposes, including to make furniture.

Bald cypress

Dogwood

Sweet goldenrod

Fauna

Gray Fox The gray fox, Delaware's official wildlife animal, is a small canid. Canids are members of a family of animals that includes wolves and dogs. The gray fox is the only canid in North America that can climb trees! Despite its name, the gray fox is born dark brown, and as an adult it has a red and white belly and legs. As a result, it is sometimes mistaken for a red fox.

Gray fox

Horseshoe Crab These crabs are a familiar sight on Delaware's beaches, where their long brown shells dot the sand. Horseshoe crabs can also be spotted swimming in the waves, which they can do upside down! While their spiky tail and spines look dangerous, they are harmless to humans. Horseshoe crabs eat worms and mollusks on the ocean floor.

Stonefly This creature is Delaware's official macroinvertebrate—an animal without a backbone that is large enough to be seen without a microscope. The population of macroinvertebrates is a sign of a healthy wetland, which is why Delaware made the choice of recognizing the stonefly. Although they have wings, stoneflies tend to walk around as they search for algae to eat.

Horseshoe crab

Tiger Swallowtail In 1999, tiger swallowtails became Delaware's state butterfly. The tiger swallowtail was chosen "because of its beautiful black and orange colors." It is a species commonly found in the woods near water, but tiger swallowtails can also be seen in towns and city parks across the state.

Weakfish This fish has a silver belly and a greenish back with black speckles. The weakfish is also called the sea trout. It is commonly caught by fishermen and can grow up to 3 feet (1 m) in length. Its importance in the fishing industry resulted in it being named Delaware's state fish.

Weakfish

Delaware's Creation

Native Americans were the first inhabitants of modern-day Delaware. They supported themselves by farming as well as hunting and fishing. They were eventually forced from their lands by European settlers. Swedes were the first to build a lasting settlement. Swedish chronicler Thomas Holm later wrote about the colony and how these early settlers saw the land:

The Swedes purchased this land at different times and by parcels from the [Native] Americans, the right owners thereof. The Bay is nine miles [14 km] in length, and six or seven miles [10 or 11 km] broad; the [Native] Americans call it Poutaxat, the English, Delaware Bay, from Monsieur Delaware, one of their captains … the Dutch call it the South River of the New Netherlands, to distinguish it from the North River, on which New Amsterdam is situated; but the Swedes call it the River of New Sweden.

The soil and climate of this country is the most pleasant and fertile in all America; it abounds with every kind of beasts, birds, fishes, valuable trees, and excellent fruits; there is not anywhere a place better suited for every kind of culture, or that agrees better with the human constitution.

This map of Swedish settlements along the Delaware River dates to 1696.

The Dutch also tried to lay claim to the region, but eventually the English took over. Modern-day Delaware became part of the new colony of Pennsylvania. However, the residents did not believe they were represented in that large state. They became independent in 1776—the same year that the United States declared its independence.

Delaware's northern border is rather strange. Rather than being a straight line or following a river, it is the arc of part of a circle. This dates to colonial times when Delaware first became part of Pennsylvania. Part of the border was defined as a circle 12 miles (19 km) around the town of New Castle.

Known as the Twelve-Mile Circle, this strange border led to trouble. Delaware claims that all the Delaware River—which forms its border with New Jersey—inside the circle belongs to it. Meanwhile, New Jersey claims half the river. The border issue is so contentious that multiple cases about it have been brought before the Supreme Court.

In 2008, New Jersey wanted to construct a natural gas terminal extending into the river, but Delaware wanted to stop it. Delaware filed a lawsuit and even considered calling up their state's National Guard to defend their claim! However, there was no need. The Supreme Court ruled in Delaware's favor and forbid the project from being built.

Delaware's
Twelve-Mile Circle

The Delaware state government passed several laws to reverse these trends. Delaware became one of the first states to establish a department of natural resources and environmental control. In 1971, the Coastal Zone Act stopped the building of any industrial plants along the state's coast.

Despite these efforts, the quality of air and water continued to decline. A government study in 1989 showed that 63 percent of Delaware's lakes, rivers, and streams were not safe for fishing or swimming. Around 80 percent of the state's people lived in areas where the air did not meet federal standards.

Delawareans and their state officials have worked hard to reduce pollution. Special "action teams" work to clean up the state's waterways. By using these teams, the government is not tackling these problems alone. The state environmental agency has asked citizens to get involved by studying the sources of pollution and coming up with strategies to reduce pollution in the state's waterways. Government agencies also closely monitor air quality around the state. Strict laws have been passed to correct and regulate a variety of environmental problems.

Clean Energy

Delawareans are also concerned about **climate change**—the slow increase in worldwide temperatures. One effect of global warming is rising sea levels. This could have a big impact on the wildlife, people, homes, and businesses in coastal areas of Delaware. The state is exploring ways to reduce the use of the fossil fuels. Burning fossil fuels, such as coal, creates energy to produce electricity, but it also contributes to climate change. "Clean" energy sources, such as wind and solar power, are better for the environment.

Delaware's efforts to expand use of green energy have been noticed. The state had twenty-nine times more solar installations in 2014 than it did in 2008. From 2008 to 2016, it increased its solar capacity from 2 megawatts to 108 megawatts to become a national leader in solar energy.

Bruce A. Henry Solar Energy Farm has sixteen thousand solar panels!

The Delaware Electric Cooperative's Bruce A. Henry Solar Energy Farm, which is close to Georgetown, was completed in the summer of 2013. It cost $14 million. There are sixteen thousand solar panels at the 20-acre (8 ha) facility, which produces enough energy to power five hundred rural Sussex homes.

In the summer of 2014, the state created a Green Energy Fund to encourage people to install small-scale solar panel systems. The fund will also increase incentives for people to use more geothermal and solar hot water systems to heat their homes.

Delaware encourages young people to get involved in helping the environment. The Young Environmentalist of the Year awards honor students who have worked to protect, restore, or improve the state's natural wonders. Any Delaware student can participate.

Delaware is also looking to wind energy to power the state. In 2011, it was set to be the first state with an offshore wind farm: a group of wind turbines in the ocean off the coast. The deal fell through, and Rhode Island became the first. However, in August of 2017, the governor of Delaware directed the state government to revisit the issue.

Delaware's Biggest Cities

(Population numbers are from the US Census Bureau's 2017 projections for incorporated cities.)

Wilmington

1. Wilmington: population 71,106

Delaware's most populous city is home to many kinds of businesses. Key industries that thrive in Wilmington include credit card companies, life insurance, banks, and legal services. DowDuPont, one of the largest chemical companies in the world, has one of its headquarters in the city.

2. Dover: population 37,538

The capital city of Delaware was a key stop on the Underground Railroad because it was a slave state near the free states of Pennsylvania and New Jersey. Dover features museums, wildlife refuges, and institutions of higher learning, like Delaware State University.

3. Newark: population 33,858

Newark is home to the University of Delaware Figure Skating Club, where some of the world's best figure skaters have trained. National, world, and Olympic champions, including some from other countries, travel to Newark to practice. Newark also boasts beloved parks and the Christiana Mall. The mall draws shoppers from out of state thanks to its many stores and Delaware's lack of sales tax.

4. Middletown: population 21,897

Middletown is one of the fastest growing places in Delaware. Between 2000 and 2010, the population of the town more than tripled. Every year, the town hosts the M.O.T. Big Ball Marathon to raise funds for charity.

5. Smyrna: population 11,584

This small town is rich in history. Smyrna was founded prior to the Revolutionary War, though it was originally called Duck Creek due to its location near the waterway of the same name. Smyrna is one of Delaware's fastest-growing municipalities.

6. Milford: population 11,075

Milford was built along the Mispillion River. To celebrate the river's role in the town's history, Milford built the Mispillion Riverwalk, where visitors can stroll and see where seven shipyards produced more than six hundred wooden sailing ships between 1680 and 1927.

Milford

7. Seaford: population 7,750

In 1939, the DuPont Company chose Seaford as the site of the first nylon plant, leading to the moniker "Nylon Capital of the World." The Seaford Museum celebrates the city's history.

8. Georgetown: population 7,291

Every two years, Georgetown hosts a holiday known as **Return Day** two days after Election Day. The event originated in colonial days, when residents would gather in the town to hear election results. Winners and losers from political races still gather for this lighthearted celebration.

Georgetown

9. Elsmere: population 6,045

During the early twentieth century, the Delaware State Fair Association purchased land in Elsmere and built fairgrounds that included a racetrack for horses, cars, and motorcycles. This area became the site of the Delaware State Fair from 1917 to 1928, when the fair moved to Harrington. Today, residents enjoy Elsmere's parks and an annual holiday parade.

10. New Castle: population 5,348

The area that would become New Castle was founded in 1651 by Peter Stuyvesant, one of the most notable leaders of Dutch settlement in the New World. New Castle is home to the First State National Historic Park.

A Lenape wigwam by the Delaware River stands as a reminder of Delaware's first residents.

2 The History of Delaware

Delaware was first inhabited by Native Americans at least 11,500 years ago. At the time, the area was very different from today. It was still covered by sheets of ice because the most recent ice age was just ending. Archaeologists have found many stone artifacts from this period that are evidence of an advanced culture composed of people who hunted extensively. Delaware's Native Americans are an important part of the state's rich history.

Early Colonization

British explorer Henry Hudson became the first European to visit the area in 1609. He had been hired by the Dutch East India Company to find a route to the Far East. Hudson briefly sailed into Delaware Bay before turning back and heading farther north up the Atlantic coast. He instead explored the river in New York that is now named for him.

The name Delaware was given to the bay and the river in 1610. English sea captain Samuel Argall named the bodies of water in honor of Sir Thomas West, Lord De La Warr. West was serving as governor of Virginia—

FAST FACT
The Lenape and Nanticoke people were the original inhabitants of modern-day Delaware before the arrival of the Europeans. They spoke related languages of the Algonquian language family. After being forced from their lands by European colonists, the two tribes intermarried.

Henry Hudson

Sir Thomas West,
Lord De La Warr

the only English colony in North America at the time. The name was later applied to the land on the western side of Delaware Bay and the southern end of the Delaware River.

Residents of the present-day town of Lewes often call their town "the first town in the first state." It was there that a group of Dutch settlers had hoped to start a colony in 1631. That early settlement was named Zwaanendael, which means "valley of the swans." The settlement lasted less than two years. After a misunderstanding over stolen property, the Lenape destroyed the settlement and killed all the colonists. That massacre would be the only warfare between Native Americans and European colonists in Delaware.

In 1638, a group of Swedish settlers built Fort Christina near present-day Wilmington. They named the fort and a nearby river for the eleven-year-old queen of Sweden. The new colony, named New Sweden, also included settlers from Finland. The leader and first governor of the colony was a Dutchman named Peter Minuit. He had been dismissed as the governor of New Netherland (which included present-day New York). The Swedish colony continued to grow. By 1644, settlers from Sweden and Finland were living on both sides of the Delaware River. The settlers made a permanent contribution to American life by constructing the first log cabins in America. American pioneers would build these simple structures for the next 250 years.

The Dutch knew that the Delaware River and Delaware Bay were important for trade and shipping. They wanted to gain control of the area. In 1651, they built Fort Casimir at the future site of the city of New Castle. The Swedes drove them out in 1654, but the Dutch stormed back and took over the fort and Fort

Christina in 1655. Dutch control did not last long either. In 1664, a powerful English fleet chartered by James, Duke of York and brother to Britain's King Charles II, sailed into Delaware Bay and quickly forced the Dutch to surrender.

In 1681, to satisfy a debt, King Charles II of England gave a huge tract of land to William Penn, who established the colony of Pennsylvania. However, the new colony did not have any waterways that led to the ocean. To solve that problem, the English gave Penn the land around the Delaware River. The area became known as the Lower Counties of Pennsylvania. The people in the three counties—New Castle, Kent, and Sussex—did not think they had enough say in the Pennsylvania government. In 1704, Penn agreed to let the Lower Counties set up their own assembly.

The town of New Castle became the capital of the Lower Counties. Today, a visual reminder of Delaware's unique history can be seen there. The New Castle Court House displays the flags of all four nations that controlled the area at different times—Sweden, the Netherlands, Great Britain, and the United States.

Between 1763 and 1767, surveyors named Charles Mason and Jeremiah Dixon drew the boundary that would become known as the Mason-Dixon Line. The line's purpose was originally to settle a land dispute between British colonies in Maryland and Pennsylvania (including land in Delaware). The Mason-Dixon Line became important again in the years leading up to and during the Civil War. It served as a symbolic marker between the states to the north that abolished slavery and those to the south where slavery remained legal. Today, the line is still referred to as a cultural boundary between the North and South.

This map of Zwaanendael was made in 1639.

Fort Christina is open to visitors from Memorial Day to Labor Day.

A monument marks the Mason-Dixon Line.

Important People in Delaware's History

Richard Allen

Annie Jump Cannon

Henry Heimlich

Richard Allen

Born into slavery in Philadelphia in 1760, Richard Allen was soon sold with his family to a farmer in Delaware. As a young man, he bought his own freedom and became involved in the Methodist Society. He later founded the African Methodist Episcopal Church so that African Americans could worship free from prejudices of white church leaders. It was the first African American church in the country.

Annie Jump Cannon

An important astronomer, Annie Jump Cannon was raised in Dover, Delaware. She graduated from Wellesley College and went on to work at the Harvard College Observatory, where she changed how stars were categorized. Her work was so important she was the first woman to receive an honorary doctorate from Oxford University.

Éleuthère Irénée du Pont

The first of the du Pont family to come to the United States, E. I. du Pont was born in Paris. He immigrated to the United States in 1800, and within two years he founded Eleutherian Mills, a gunpowder mill in Delaware. It became the most important source of gunpowder in America and was the start of the du Ponts' massive family business.

Henry Heimlich

Doctor Henry Heimlich was born in Wilmington, Delaware, in 1920. He became a physician and invented the Heimlich maneuver that is used to help people who are choking. This innovative treatment has saved tens of thousands of lives around the globe.

William Julius "Judy" Johnson

Third baseman Judy Johnson is remembered as one of the best players of the African American baseball leagues. He was elected to the Hall of Fame in 1975. His defensive plays were renowned, and over his long career he played for three Pennsylvania teams. However, he spent much of his life in northern Delaware, where today there is a park that bears his name.

Thomas Macdonough

Orphaned at the age of twelve, Thomas Macdonough joined the US Navy as a young man. He distinguished himself with his courage under fire and rose through the ranks. He took part in fighting in North Africa in the early 1800s during the Barbary Wars. By the War of 1812, he was a master commandant, and he led a fleet to win the important Battle of Lake Champlain. Macdonough was born and raised in Delaware.

Louis L. Redding

This civil rights pioneer became the first African American lawyer in Delaware in 1929. He went on to argue important cases that helped put an end to segregation—the system of separate schools and government services for whites and minorities.

Caesar Rodney

This Delaware native was a prominent figure during the Revolutionary War. Caesar Rodney cast the tie-breaking vote in favor of Delaware supporting the Declaration of Independence. He also led Delaware's militia during the war and later served as president of Delaware (the position of governor today).

Mary Ann Shadd

The first female African American newspaper editor in North America was born in Wilmington, Delaware, in 1823. Mary Ann Shadd grew up to become a prominent **abolitionist**, someone who fought against slavery. She founded the *Provincial Freeman* newspaper for African Americans and recruited soldiers during the Civil War to fight for an end to slavery.

Delaware's Role in the Revolution

Wilmington resident John Dickinson was called "the Penman of the Revolution." From 1767 to 1768, Dickinson published a series of essays called "Letters from a Farmer in Pennsylvania." The twelve letters were widely distributed among the thirteen colonies. The essays helped unite colonists against the Townshend Acts, a series of laws governing the colonies passed by the British Parliament that were met with great resistance in America. This backlash played a major role in the lead up to the American Revolution.

President Thomas Jefferson recognized Dickinson as being "among the first of the advocates for the rights of his country when assailed by Great Britain" whose "name will be consecrated in history as one of the great worthies of the revolution."

In July 1776, the Second Continental Congress met in Philadelphia to vote on the Declaration of Independence. There was no guarantee that the declaration would be approved. Not all colonists wanted to break free from British rule. The two Delaware delegates in attendance were split. The third delegate, Caesar Rodney, was back in Delaware. When this news reached Rodney, he knew what he had to do. He rode through the night on horseback and arrived in time to break the tie in the Delaware delegation. Delaware voted for independence on July 2, and the Declaration of Independence was approved on July 4.

New Castle lawyer Thomas McKean also was an important voice in helping persuade the colonies to break away from British rule. McKean was one of Delaware's delegates to the First Continental Congress in 1774 and the Second

Continental Congress in 1775. When McKean noticed Caesar Rodney was absent from the vote on the Declaration of Independence, he requested Rodney take his famous overnight ride to cast the deciding vote.

At the Stamp Act Congress of 1765, McKean proposed a voting procedure that would have a lasting impact throughout American history: that each colony, regardless of size or population, should have one vote. The Congress of the Articles of Confederation also adopted the practice, and the principle of state equality continues in the United States Senate.

Caesar Rodney rode a horse overnight to vote "yes" on the Declaration of Independence.

In a way, Delaware's true declaration of independence had come on June 15, 1776. That's when the assembly had voted to separate from both the Pennsylvania colony and from English rule. The Lower Counties became known as Delaware State.

About four thousand soldiers from Delaware fought during the Revolution. However, only one brief battle was fought in Delaware, in September of 1777. The battle took place in what is now the city of Newark. Only seven hundred colonial soldiers fought in the battle, and the British easily fought them back and took control of the region.

Immediately after the battle, the British defeated George Washington's forces at

The Original Americans

A Nanticoke dancer attends the Nanticoke Powwow in Millsboro in 2012.

For many years before the first Europeans arrived, the land of modern-day Delaware was home to small bands of Native Americans. The largest group was the Lenape, whom European settlers later called the Delaware. The Lenape lived in small villages close to the Delaware River and Delaware Bay. The men hunted and fished, and the women tended crops, prepared meals, and handled most of the childcare. A smaller tribe called the Nanticoke lived to the south and west, closer to Chesapeake Bay. The cultures of the Nanticoke and Lenape tribes are intertwined in many ways. While each group has their own region and way of living, they share many traditions and much of their history.

Both the Nanticoke and the Lenape relied heavily on farming to feed the tribe. Corn, beans, and squash were important crops for both groups. In addition, both the Nanticoke and the Lenape hunted animals such as bear, deer, turkeys, and geese. Each tribe used shells and beads in colorful traditional art and jewelry. The family unit was very important to both groups as well, with strong ties being valued between parents and children.

European settlement had a significant impact on the history of both tribes. In 1684, settlers and Nanticoke reached an agreement to create a reservation in Maryland where much of the tribe could live. However, nonnative people continued to move onto this land, so in 1707 the Nanticoke purchased 3,000 acres (1,214 ha) on Broad Creek in Delaware. Continued resettlement eventually led to many Nanticoke moving to neighboring states and beyond. The Lenape faced similar trials, and many scattered across the eastern United States as a result of conflict with European settlers, intertribal fighting, and disease.

Today, a small number of both Lenape and Nanticoke people remain in Delaware. The Lenape have been a state-recognized tribe in Delaware since 2016. The Nanticoke Indian Association of Millsboro has been a state-recognized tribe in Delaware since 1881. The last person speaking the Nanticoke language died in 1856. A large number of people from both tribes now live in Oklahoma, Pennsylvania, New Jersey, and parts of Canada. Though the Lenape population is largely diminished in Delaware, many who migrated to Oklahoma became part of the now federally recognized Delaware Nation.

Spotlight on the Nanticoke

In Algonquian, the common language of Northeastern tribes, the word Nanticoke means "the tidewater people."

Clans: The Nanticoke people were closely related to several tribes: the Choptank, the Assateague, the Piscataway, and the Doeg.

Homes: The Nanticoke people built wigwams, dome-shaped homes made of wood, tree bark, and animal hide. Larger dwellings called longhouses were used for tribal gatherings.

Food: Farming was an important part of life for the Nanticoke. Corn, beans, squash, pumpkins, sunflowers, and tobacco were some of the crops they grew. They also gathered nuts and berries, and fished for clams, oysters, crabs, and more. Nanticoke men hunted small animals including ducks, geese, squirrels, and deer.

Clothing: Nanticoke people made pants, skirts and coats from animal hide and fur to survive cold winters. Decorations and jewelry were made from shells, beads, and feathers. Sometimes they used berries to tattoo or paint their skin.

Art: The Nanticoke created colorful jewelry, beadwork, and pottery. Like many other tribes, they made **wampum**, or beads made from shells.

These buildings are part of the original du Pont gunpowder mill.

Brandywine Creek, a few miles away in Pennsylvania. The British followed this success by launching a surprise attack against Wilmington and managed to capture the president of Delaware, whose position was similar to the governor today. The Delaware state government moved south from nearby New Castle to Dover for safety. Dover has been Delaware's capital ever since.

The colonies won their independence in 1783. A Constitutional Convention was held in Philadelphia in the summer of 1787. The new Constitution had to be ratified, or accepted, by nine of the thirteen states before it could take effect. Each state held a special convention to debate and vote on the Constitution. On December 7, Delaware became the first state to approve it.

After Independence

For much of its history, Delaware was mainly a farming state. The fast-moving streams and rivers provided waterpower for mills. These mills made Delaware an important center for processing flour and other foods that were sold in nearby cities, especially Philadelphia and Baltimore. In 1802, the du Pont family started a gunpowder mill on the banks of Brandywine Creek near Wilmington. The family founded the company just two years after fleeing France to escape the French Revolution. Throughout the 1800s and early 1900s, the DuPont mills produced most of the nation's gunpowder. The site of their original plant, called Eleutherian Mills, is now an expansive museum called the Hagley Museum and Library.

Trade and manufacturing gradually became more important to Delaware. The state's mills

One tradition that is unique to Delaware is Return Day. Every other year, local election results are announced in the small town of Georgetown. Residents from all over the county gather to hear the town crier call them out. Winning and losing candidates parade through the town side by side while people celebrate with food and drink.

Politicians bury a hatchet each Return Day.

The tradition dates to at least the 1800s, perhaps even the 1700s. It still occurs two days after voting because election results used to take two days to travel south from Dover to Georgetown. In those early days, free ox roast sandwiches were distributed to people who came. People even dressed up in outlandish outfits, similar to Mardi Gras today. Nowadays, the atmosphere of Return Day is festive but not over the top.

The purpose of Return Day is to bring people together after divisive elections. Candidates from both parties shake hands and parade together in solidarity. There is even a symbolic burying of a real hatchet. ("To bury the hatchet" is a phrase that means to stop an argument.) This unique tradition of southern Delaware is a lesson in civility in politics.

Return Day

produced not only flour and gunpowder but also a variety of other products, including cloth and paper. The city of Wilmington became a center for both manufacturing and trade. The methods for transporting goods in and out of Delaware improved. In 1829, the Chesapeake and Delaware Canal was opened. The canal reduced the water route from Philadelphia to Baltimore by nearly 300 miles (485 km). From the late 1830s on, railroads steadily grew in importance, and water transportation declined.

In the 1860s, tensions between the North and the South led to the Civil War (1861–1865). Eleven Southern states broke away from the rest of the country and formed the Confederate States of America. One of the main reasons for the war was slavery. The first slaves brought to the British North American colonies that became the United States had been abducted from Africa in the 1600s. By the mid-1800s, Southern farmers relied on slaves as field workers. However, most states in the North did not allow slavery by this time.

Delaware struggled with the issue of slavery. In 1860, about twenty thousand free African Americans lived in the state. Many white Delawareans wanted to see slavery abolished, or ended. Some helped slaves on the Underground Railroad—a secret network of people who helped slaves escape to freedom in the years before the Civil War. Some Delaware homes and meeting houses served as "stations," or safe hiding places, for slaves on their journey north. Thomas Garrett was Delaware's most famous "conductor" on the Underground Railroad. Before the Civil War ended, he helped more than 2,700 slaves escape to freedom. He was arrested and fined in 1848, but he refused to give up his fight against slavery.

Garrett was the inspiration for one of the main characters in *Uncle Tom's Cabin*, a book by Harriet Beecher Stowe that helped fuel the abolitionist movement with its antislavery message.

The general attitude at the time seemed to establish a pattern that New Castle County in the north was mostly antislavery, and Sussex County in the south was proslavery. Several attempts were made to abolish slavery in Delaware. In 1792, lawmakers tried to make a ban on slavery part of the new state constitution but failed. Bills to abolish slavery were introduced in the Delaware General Assembly in 1796 and 1797. In 1803, an attempt at gradual emancipation—slowly phasing slavery out— was ended by the Speaker of the state house of representatives, who cast the tiebreaking vote. Further attempts were made, but none passed.

Thomas Garrett was Delaware's most famous Underground Railroad "conductor."

At the beginning of the Civil War, there were 1,800 slaves in Delaware. Though Delaware stayed in the Union when the Civil War began, several hundred of its people fought for the Confederacy. After nearly four years of bloody battles, the Confederacy surrendered in the spring of 1865, and the country was unified once again. The Thirteenth Amendment to the US Constitution officially abolished slavery nationwide in December 1865. Yet many decades would pass before African Americans in Delaware, and other states, would truly have equal rights.

After the war, large numbers of immigrants came to work in the factories in and near Wilmington. This allowed industry to thrive in Delaware. The southern part of Delaware maintained a strong agricultural economy, with corn and wheat being the main crops.

Dancing Corn

Corn is Delaware's most important crop. Fields of it can be seen driving through the state. This experiment uses corn kernels to explore the scientific concept of density.

Supplies

- A large glass jar
- ¼ cup of corn kernels
- 3 cups of water
- 3 tablespoons of baking soda
- ½ cup of vinegar

Directions

1. Put the water and baking soda in the jar and stir until the baking soda has dissolved.
2. Add the corn kernels to the mixture.
3. Slowly add the vinegar. The mixture will start bubbling. If it looks like the jar is going to overflow, add the vinegar more slowly.
4. When the baking soda and vinegar come into contact, there is a chemical reaction. The gas carbon dioxide is formed. This gas is less dense than water. Density is the measure of how much space something takes up in relation to its weight. If something is less dense than water, it will float. If it is denser, it will sink.
5. The corn is denser, so it sinks to the bottom of the jar. However, the carbon dioxide is less dense, so it floats. When the carbon dioxide sticks to the corn, it brings the corn to the surface with it as it floats up. The result is corn that looks like it is dancing!

The World Wars

In the twentieth century, industry changed in many ways—and the lives of Delawareans changed with it. The use of new sources of power, including steam and electricity, led to new industries in the Wilmington area. In addition to gunpowder, factories made ships, railroad cars, and machinery. These industries were important for America during World War I (in which the United States fought from 1917 to 1918) and World War II (in which the United States fought from 1941 to 1945).

A woman works in a factory during World War II.

The Great Depression—a time of widespread economic hardship across the United States during the 1930s—had a great impact on Delaware's economy. Factories and businesses closed, leaving thousands of workers unemployed. However, Delaware suffered less than other states because of its strong agricultural industry.

Delaware's shoreline played an important role in World War II. Between 1939 and 1942, eleven triangulation towers were built on the coast of Delaware, in an area stretching 40 miles (64 km). Soldiers would man the towers for any sightings of enemy vessels. Because so many important sites of American industry existed in

This World War II triangulation tower is in Cape Henlopen State Park.

this area—chemical plants in Wilmington and Philadelphia's shipyard are two examples—it was considered a critically important area to protect.

These threats were very real, as German submarines sank American ships off the East Coast, and survivors of these attacks often ended up on Delaware's shores. One German submarine surrendered off one of the stations, Fort Miles, in 1945.

The towers were built to last twenty years, but some still stand today and are expected to last another half-century. Visitors can climb some of the towers, including the one at popular Cape Henlopen State Park, for spectacular views of Delaware and the Atlantic Ocean.

DuPont supplied much of the gunpowder used by Americans and their allies. The company continued to flourish in the early twentieth century and moved into manufacturing dynamite and smokeless powder. DuPont purchased several smaller chemical companies, and in 1912 these actions caught the attention of the American government. The Sherman Antitrust Act was a federal law that barred companies from becoming anticompetitive—meaning they were so big that other companies were unable to compete against them. Under the act, the courts declared that DuPont had a monopoly, or an unfair amount of control, in the explosives business and ordered them to split into smaller companies.

In spite of these challenges, DuPont continued to grow and established two of the first industrial laboratories in the United States. These are laboratories where scientists work to develop new products for a company to sell. The DuPont labs were key to the company's expansion into products that were not explosives.

In 1914, DuPont invested in General Motors (GM), helping the fledgling automotive

DuPont's headquarters in Wilmington in 2015. That year, DuPont merged with Dow and became DowDuPont.

company survive. Pierre S. du Pont, one of DuPont's owners, became president of GM. Under his leadership, GM became the number-one automotive maker in the world. In 1957, the US Supreme Court ruled against DuPont, declaring that its investment in GM was considered a monopoly. The government forced DuPont to give up the large amount of stock it owned in the car company.

The increased production in factories and shipyards during World War II provided jobs for many Delawareans. While many men fought overseas, women in the United States served their country by working in factories and other industries that helped the war effort. Many Delawarean women worked at jobs that were available only to men before the war.

Delaware has continued to change since World War II. DuPont moved toward producing chemicals for paints and other

FAST FACT
The 2008 financial
crisis and the
Great Recession
it helped cause
were a large blow
to Delaware's
economy.
Unemployment
in Delaware
doubled with the
economic crisis.
Furthermore,
wages also shrank
in Delaware
between 2008 and
2015. It was the
only state in the
country where
this was the case.

household products. Most of the "heavy" industries have been replaced by "light" industries, which make such products as processed foods, medical instruments, and electronic components. Today, Delawareans try to continue to adapt to changing times.

Delaware Looks to the Future

In recent years, Delaware has looked to improve life for children and youths in the state. Governor Jack Markell made education reform a priority during his time in office between 2009 and 2017. One of his first goals was to qualify for the Race to the Top program.

Race to the Top was a competition between states to receive money from the federal government to spend on education reform. States tried to demonstrate that they were making progress and would use the money effectively. In 2010, the first money was distributed, and just two states out of forty qualified. One was Delaware. It received $119 million to improve its schools.

Building on that success, Markell began the new World Language Expansion Initiative in 2011. This program allows thousands of elementary school students in Delaware to learn Spanish and Mandarin Chinese in immersion classes. Half of the school day they are taught in English, while the other half they are taught in the other language. This initiative will help Delawareans compete in the global economy of modern times.

Governor John Carney

Markell's reform succeeded in many areas. The high school dropout rate in the 2011–2012 school year was 3.9 percent. By 2017, it had declined to just 1.7 percent. In 2017, the state's graduation rate also hit an all-time high. However, some parents and teachers felt that the reforms took too much power away from local schools in favor of statewide policies.

In 2017, John Carney was sworn in as the state's next governor. He, too, has made education a priority. One of his signature acts was to sign an executive order reestablishing the Juvenile Justice Advisory Group. This panel of experts is tasked with examining how to keep young people in school and out of the criminal justice system. It is the latest push to make Delaware a supportive state for all children.

Education is important to Delawareans. Here, students work on a lesson at Marbrook Elementary School.

3 Who Lives in Delaware?

As of July 2016, 62 percent of Delawareans were non-Hispanic white, 23 percent were African American, 9 percent were Hispanic, and 4 percent were Asian, while 2.6 percent of people identified as more than one race. The north of the state around Wilmington tends to be more diverse than the largely white Sussex County in the south. Delawareans celebrate their differences and are brought together by their love for their home state.

Early History

The makeup of Delaware's population changed a great deal during the 1700s. One change was the sharp decline in the Native American population. Many Lenape (later known as the Delaware) died from diseases brought by Europeans, such as **smallpox**. Much of the Native Americans' land was taken over by European settlers. Most of the indigenous people in Delaware moved west, joining other tribes beyond the Appalachian Mountains. By 1750, only a few thousand Native Americans remained in Delaware.

FAST FACT

Many people from all over the world call Delaware home. About 9 percent of Delawareans were born outside of the United States. This is slightly under the national average of 13 percent, but it's still a considerable number. The most common countries of birth are Mexico and India.

This painting shows Native Americans meeting Swedish settlers in Delaware in 1638.

Today, Delaware's Native Americans, including members of the Nanticoke and Lenape tribes, make up 0.6 percent of the state's population, or about 5,600 people. Many of the Nanticoke live in central Delaware.

European Settlement

As the Native American population declined, the white population increased. The 1700s brought newcomers called the Scots-Irish; these people came from the area that today is known as Northern Ireland. In the 1800s, troubles in Europe brought two new groups. Starting in the 1820s, large numbers of immigrants came from Ireland, seeking to escape poverty. Immigration from Ireland increased further in the 1840s, when disease destroyed the potato crop—the main source of food for most poor families in Ireland. Large numbers of German immigrants arrived in the 1840s and 1850s, driven from their homeland by political unrest. Like many immigrants, both groups faced prejudice from many native-born Americans. By about 1900, however, both groups had integrated into the mainstream of American life.

In the late 1800s, the development of industry, especially in and around Wilmington, drew a new wave of immigrants from southern and eastern Europe. Poles, Slavs, Jews, Italians, and other groups arrived. They found work in factories and on the railroads.

A Religious Melting Pot

The first European settlers represented different Protestant religions. Protestants are Christians who do not recognize the supremacy of the Pope—the head of the Catholic faith. The

Peach Pie Recipe

Delaware's state dessert is peach pie. It is quite easy to make yourself with some ripe peaches and a pie crust.

Ingredients

- One store-bought pie crust
- 6 ripe peaches
- ¾ cup of sugar
- 1 tablespoon of lemon juice
- ¼ teaspoon of nutmeg
- ¼ cup of flour

Directions

1. Begin preheating the oven to the temperature on the pie crust packaging.
2. Peel the peaches. Remove their pits and dice them into small pieces on a cutting board.
3. Stir the flour, nutmeg, and sugar together in a mixing bowl.
4. Add the peaches and lemon juice. Gently mix the ingredients together with your hands.
5. Prepare the pie crust as the packaging directs, and add the pie filling you have made. Cook it for the length of time that the packaging says.
6. Once it has cooled, enjoy your peach pie!

William Penn, founder of Pennsylvania

Dutch belonged to the Dutch Reform Church, and the Swedes were mostly Lutheran. Many English settlers were members of another Protestant group, the Episcopal Church. Small groups of Quakers also came to Delaware from Pennsylvania. Pennsylvania's founder, William Penn, was a Quaker. The Quakers were members of the Religious Society of Friends. Although few in number, the Quakers had a strong influence in Delaware. They strongly opposed slavery—in Delaware and in the rest of the United States.

The 1700s and 1800s saw the arrival of large numbers of Presbyterians and Roman Catholics. In the late 1700s, traveling preachers helped spread the beliefs of Methodism. The Methodist Episcopal Church soon became the largest in Delaware. Today, Roman Catholics and Methodists are the two biggest religious groups in the state.

Public Education

For many years, education was not unified throughout the state. While the early colonists valued education, most schools were operated by local churches, and the quality of the education was uneven. In about 1700, wealthy English families began sending their sons to schools in England. They educated their daughters at home or at boarding schools in Philadelphia.

Delaware established a fund for schools in 1796, but the money was not used for years. In 1829, a new law set up the state's first true public-school system. Still, the quality of education in many schools was poor. Conditions were even worse for African American students, who were not allowed to attend the same schools as white children. In the 1920s, a member of the du Pont family donated a large sum of his own money to

FAST FACT

Nearly one in four Delawareans is African American. This makes it the ninth-highest state for percentage of African Americans in the country. Within Delaware, most African Americans live in the densely populated New Castle and Kent counties. The percentage of African Americans in rural Sussex county is about half of the state average— 12.5 percent.

University of Delaware

Delaware's Biggest Colleges and Universities

(Enrollment numbers are from *US News and World Report* 2018 and 2019 college rankings.)

1. University of Delaware, Newark
(18,946 undergraduate students, 2019)

2. Wilmington University, New Castle
(8,460 undergraduate students, 2019)

3. Delaware State University, Dover
(4,050 undergraduate students, 2019)

4. Wesley College, Dover
(1,345 undergraduate students, 2018)

5. Goldey-Beacom College, Wilmington
(698 undergraduate students, 2018)

Delaware State University

Goldey-Beacom College's seal

Rev. Dr. Francis Alison ran a school that later became the University of Delaware.

improve the schools. Much of the money went to build new schools for African Americans.

In 1954, the Supreme Court ruled that schools could no longer be segregated. All schools must be open to black students as well as white students. Two legal cases that became part of the famous *Brown v. Board of Education* case that ended segregation started in Delaware courts. However, schools in some Delaware cities, especially Wilmington, did not want to change. In 1978, the city started a court-ordered program to integrate the schools. Black students from Wilmington were bused to schools in the suburbs. White students from the suburbs were bused to schools in the city.

Delaware is home to two well-known public universities. Founded in 1743, the University of Delaware is the oldest college in the state. The Presbytery of Lewes sent out a petition that said there was a need for an educated clergy. The first class of the Rev. Dr. Francis Alison's new school included three men who would sign the Declaration of Independence: Thomas McKean, George Read, and James Smith. Read also was among those who signed the Constitution of the United States.

A women's college opened in 1914, and in 1921 it merged with the school founded by Dr. Alison. The two colleges became the University of Delaware. Today, about eighteen thousand undergraduate students are enrolled at the school.

Delaware State University is a historically black college that was founded in 1891, and it has an enrollment of about four thousand undergraduate students. Among its most famous graduates are trumpet player and composer Clifford Brown, football player and Super Bowl winner John Taylor, American diplomat Dr. Clyde Bishop, and bank executive David G. Turner.

The Twentieth and Twenty-First Centuries

America's involvement in World War I and World War II led to a sharp increase in city populations, especially in Wilmington. Large numbers of people, including many African Americans from the South, came to work in the factories and shipyards.

Kent County is known for its farms.

After World War II, many people left Wilmington for its suburbs. Many newcomers to the state also moved to the suburbs. Today, about half of Delaware's people live within commuting distance of Wilmington.

Delaware experienced its largest population growth from 1950 to 1960. The continued development of the state's chemical industry drew scientists, technicians, and other workers from other parts of the United States and from other countries.

Most of southern Delaware remains rural. The area's population is also diverse—Kent County, for example, is home to prosperous dairy and potato farms operated by Polish American families who moved from Long Island, New York. At Iron Hill, there is a large group of people from Finland who came after World War I. A small Amish settlement lies near Dover. The Amish people are a Christian sect. They have a simple lifestyle on farms and do not rely on modern machinery.

In the early twenty-first century, Delaware's diversity is increasing at a faster rate than the national average. By 2060, Delaware is expected to be the fourteenth most racially diverse state in the country. It is expected that the Hispanic community will grow the fastest. This diversity is a great asset for the state, as people from different cultures and backgrounds all work together to improve their community.

Delaware's Celebrities

Valerie Bertinelli

This Wilmington native got her break in show business in 1975 at just fifteen years of age when she starred in the sitcom *One Day at a Time*. Today, she is still a well-known actress. Valerie Bertinelli hosts her own show, *Valerie's Home Cooking*, on the Food Network.

Beau Biden

Beau Biden

Born in Wilmington, Beau Biden was the oldest son of prominent politician Joe Biden. In 2006, the younger Biden was elected as Delaware's attorney general—the chief law enforcement officer. He planned to seek election as Delaware's governor in the 2016 election, but he died from brain cancer during the race.

Delino DeShields

Ryan Phillippe

Before going pro, Delino DeShields played baseball for Seaford High School. DeShields was drafted into the major leagues in 1987. Over the course of his MLB career, he played for five teams, including the Los Angeles Dodgers and the Chicago Cubs. Since his retirement as a player in 2002, DeShields has worked as a manager and coach. Two of his children are professional athletes: Delino DeShields Jr. plays for the Texas Rangers, and Diamond DeShields is a member of the Chicago Sky, a WNBA team.

Paul Goldschmidt

Major League Baseball star Paul Goldschmidt was born in Wilmington in 1987. He was drafted by the Arizona Diamondbacks in 2009. Goldschmidt, known by the nickname "Goldy," is a talented first baseman.

Ryan Phillippe

Actor Ryan Phillippe was born in New Castle. His first major role was on the soap opera *One Life to Live*, but he soon starred in many

Hollywood movies. His marriage to actress Reese Witherspoon increased his fame, and he has also produced and directed several projects.

Aubrey Plaza

Actress Aubrey Plaza spent her childhood in Wilmington. After graduating from New York University's Tisch School of the Arts, she starred in the sitcom *Parks and Recreation*. More recently, she appeared in the show *Legion*, which is part of the X-Men franchise.

Aubrey Plaza

Judge Reinhold

A native of Wilmington, Judge Reinhold has had a long career in Hollywood, starting in 1979. He has been in more than seventy-five television shows and movies. One of his most famous appearances was in all three *Beverly Hills Cop* movies alongside Eddie Murphy.

Elisabeth Shue

After spending her childhood in Delaware, actress Elisabeth Shue moved out of state to go to first Wellesley College and then Harvard University. Just before graduating from college, she dropped out to pursue her promising acting career. She has starred in many movies and television shows since then, but in 1997 she returned to Harvard and earned her degree.

Chuck Wicks

Country star Chuck Wicks grew up on a farm in Smyrna. He moved to Nashville, Tennessee, to pursue his dream of being a musician. After years of hard work, writing songs during the day and parking cars at night, he signed a contract with a record company and became a star. Wicks is known for hits like "Stealing Cinderella," "All I Ever Wanted," and "Man of the House," which have all been top-thirty songs on the Billboard "Hot Country" chart.

Changing Demographics

Many different immigrant groups have shaped Delaware's history. They have left their mark on the state's culture. The first European colonists to come to Delaware were from Sweden, Finland, and the Netherlands. However, they never settled in the area in large numbers. After Great Britain gained control of the area, English settlers poured into the region in the 1700s. They soon outnumbered the Swedish, Finnish, and Dutch minorities. Later, small numbers of Quakers, a Protestant group persecuted in England, also came to Delaware, although most settled in Pennsylvania.

During the eighteenth century, many European groups other than the English also settled the region in smaller numbers. The Scots-Irish were one group that came in significant numbers. Like the English, they were largely Protestant. The Scots-Irish were originally from Scotland. They settled in Ireland before then coming to the United States in large numbers.

In the mid-nineteenth century, large numbers of Irish and German immigrants began arriving along the East Coast, including in Delaware. Unlike previous immigrants, the Irish were mostly Catholic. This led to conflict with the largely Protestant population. In 1854, the American Party (or "Know Nothing" movement), a national phenomenon, swept the state and claimed the governorship. It was founded largely on anti-immigrant and anti-Catholic sentiment. However, it soon lost its popularity, and eventually Protestants and Catholics in Delaware lived in harmony.

By the 1900s, many other immigrant groups were also arriving in Delaware, including Russians, Jews, Italians, and Poles. These groups brought their own unique cultures, and Delaware was a diverse and dynamic community.

Today, immigration continues to shape Delaware's population. Immigrants from around the world move to the state. Additionally, people from other states also move to Delaware to find a new home. In fact, about 44 percent of Delaware's people were born in a different US state, especially nearby Maryland, Pennsylvania, New Jersey, or New York! Many of these people from out of state are retirees who choose to come to Delaware to live out their golden years.

Meanwhile, many young people choose to leave Delaware to seek work in other states. As of 2016, about 61 percent of people born in Delaware now live somewhere else. This pull of older people into the state and push of younger people out has shifted the age of Delaware's population. With a median age of 39.6, it has the tenth-oldest population in the country.

Retirees are a growing population in Delaware.

Tourism is a large part of Delaware's economy. Here, tourists enjoy the Rehoboth Beach boardwalk.

4 At Work in Delaware

Delawareans work all sorts of jobs. Despite the state's small size, it is home to many kinds of work. Farms cover much of Sussex County in the south, while the hospitality industry thrives in beach towns along the coast. In the north, manufacturing, banking, and education all provide many jobs. The First State is well known for its business-friendly policies.

Delaware's Early Economy

The early settlers of Delaware built their farms and plantations close to the rivers and streams to make use of the waterways for transportation. There were few roads in Delaware until the 1900s, so transportation by horse-drawn vehicles was slow. Boats or sailing ships were more convenient.

In the colonial years, many of Delaware's farms and plantations grew tobacco. Ships picked up the product from the docks and transported it to markets in Europe. Tobacco rapidly wore out the soil, however, and Delawareans searched for new sources of farm income. Many in the

FAST FACT
Seaside resort towns like Rehoboth Beach and Bethany Beach are an important facet of Delaware's economy. Tourists from across the East Coast visit during the summer to bask in the sun and enjoy the peaceful surroundings. Tourists spend their money across the state and support businesses in Delaware while they relax.

A farm along the Delaware River in the 1800s

northern part of the state turned to wheat. Corn became the major crop in southern Delaware.

In the 1800s, the growing and selling of peaches created a great wave of prosperity for the state's farmers. The crops were shipped by the waterways. After 1840, they were sent by railroad to city markets, especially in Philadelphia and New York. Peach tree orchards in the state included more than eight hundred thousand trees. However, the peaches were stricken by a **blight**, or disease, called the yellows, and the orchards declined steadily after 1900. Peach growing picked up after World War II. Today, Delaware growers produce about 2 million pounds (907,200 kilograms) of peaches each year.

Peaches are an important crop in the First State.

Agriculture

The development of industry, beginning in the late 1800s, became a larger source of income. However, farming has remained very important. As the peach orchards declined, many farmers turned to growing other fruits and vegetables. Crops such as beans, peas, tomatoes, berries, and melons were shipped by water or rail. Today these farms are called "**truck farms**," since road transportation has replaced railroads and ships to move the farm products to market. Many truck farms are operated by part-time farmers.

Today, Delaware's farm industry continues to thrive. The state is home to about 2,500 farms that cover 500,000 acres (200,000 ha). Sussex

This chicken lives on a Milford farm.

County is one of the wealthiest agricultural counties in the country. Chicken broilers are Delaware's biggest farm product. Delaware farmers raise nearly 260 million chickens for their meat. Yet this important industry started by accident. In the early 1920s, Cecile and Wilmer Steele of Ocean View ordered fifty chickens. They wanted to raise the chickens and sell their eggs. But when the Steeles received five hundred chickens by mistake, they decided to raise them for their meat. Delaware's broiler industry was born.

In addition to corn and wheat, soybeans have become a major crop. Farm families in the extreme south also make holly wreaths during the Christmas season. Dairy and cattle farms are key parts of the farming economy as well.

Commercial fishing remains profitable, although pollution problems have reduced the number of fishing boats. Fishing boats and chartered boats are used to catch saltwater fish in Delaware Bay and the ocean. Additionally, shellfish harvesting along the coast is profitable.

These tour boats and fishing boats are docked in Lewes.

The DuPont Company

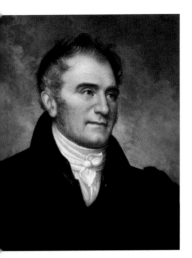

E. I. du Pont lived from 1771 to 1834.

One of the most important people in Delaware's history was an immigrant from Paris, France. Éleuthère Irénée du Pont de Nemours arrived in the United States in 1800. He had some experience making gunpowder in France. When he saw the poor quality of American gunpowder at that time, he realized it was an opportunity. He persuaded his father to finance the building of a mill to manufacture gunpowder.

The high quality of the product made the company a great success. It rapidly became the country's largest supplier of gunpowder and one of the largest in the world. Since the early 1800s, DuPont has been a mainstay of Delaware's economy. The family no longer owns the company. However, family members in each generation have been major figures in state culture and politics.

In 1912, the federal government ruled that the DuPont Company was a monopoly in the manufacture of gunpowder. A monopoly is a company that controls so much of an industry that it has no competition. As a result, DuPont was divided into three corporations: Atlas, Hercules, and DuPont.

In the early twentieth century, DuPont moved away from gunpowder production. The company began to focus on the development of chemical products, such as paints and dyes. In the mid-1930s, Wallace Carothers and other DuPont chemists developed nylon. This was a major breakthrough for the company. Nylon was used as a fabric to make parachutes and other products. Its most popular use was in women's stockings.

The DuPont laboratories and a manufacturing plant helped make Wilmington an important industrial center. The city has been called the "chemical capital of the world."

DuPont Shapes the World

DuPont's inventions have changed the world we live in. The company is responsible for inventing several materials that we use every day, from Teflon to Spandex. One of the earliest synthetic fibers DuPont created was nylon. The fiber was made from chemicals found in petroleum. First produced in 1935, it was soon incorporated into many different household products, from toothbrushes to carpets.

Nylon was strong and stretchable. It was also much cheaper to produce than its all-natural rival, silk. Nylon even proved invaluable in World War II. Parachutes and tents were made from the new material that did not rot like natural fibers. It was so useful that the government briefly forbade it from being used for nonmilitary purposes.

Nylon also sparked a wave of new synthetic fibers being invented. One that you may have heard of is **Kevlar**, a synthetic fiber so strong it is used to stop bullets. For its weight, it is five times stronger than steel. Kevlar, too, was invented by DuPont scientists. It is used not only in bulletproof vests and helmets, but also for other uses where its incredible strength, lightness, and fire-resistance are needed, including in airplanes and ships.

Marines wear Kevlar helmets during a 2014 exercise.

The Biopharmaceutical Sector

Biopharmaceutical research is a growing field that will bring jobs to Delaware.

The University of Delaware (UD) is positioning itself to be a leader in the new field of biopharmaceuticals. This field uses living cells to create drugs or treatments for diseases. Experts hope that it will treat or cure many common diseases like Alzheimer's and cancer. Before this new field can reach its potential, a great deal more research needs to be done. Delaware is stepping up to play its part.

In 2017, UD began construction of a massive biopharmaceutical research center. It is expected to bring 1,500 new jobs to northern Delaware. Experts from around the country will be hired to teach and research. University staff hope that it will make Delaware the top state when it comes to this exciting and growing new field.

The building is on a site that used to house a car manufacturing plant that closed in 2009. The construction of the new high-tech center is a symbol of hope and promise. It will likely bring biopharmaceutical manufacturing jobs to the area. As the world economy changes, Delaware is investing money in its institutions and people to adapt and remain at the forefront of innovation.

The city's location is also ideal for business. Waterways, railroads, and highways place northern Delaware within easy reach of Philadelphia; Washington, DC; and other cities.

A Diverse Economy

There is much more to industry in Delaware than chemicals, of course. Food processing is a big part of the state's economy. Large plants in Dover, for example, make gelatin, puddings, and other dessert products. Other plants in northern Delaware make baked goods, fish products, and soft drinks. Poultry processing is also an important industry.

Dover Air Force Base

Many farms across the state raise hogs. Hog farms sell their livestock to companies all over the state and throughout the country. Some of the livestock is sent to meat processing plants in Delaware. The hogs are used for ham, bacon, and other pork products.

The completion of the Delaware Memorial Bridge in 1951 linked Delaware with New Jersey. Major automobile companies soon set up assembly plants in Delaware, though changing times mean that there aren't any big auto plants in the state today.

In Delaware, government is a major source of employment. Many people have jobs in state and local government offices, in public school systems, and at the US military's Dover Air Force Base.

For a small state, Delaware has a great deal to offer tourists. Visitors enjoy the state's beaches and the clear waters of the bay, rivers, lakes, and streams. The parks and forests are excellent for hiking, mountain biking, camping, and bird-watching. Others come to the state to see the historic sites that honor Delaware's—and the nation's—history.

Dover International Speedway seats more than eighty thousand racing fans.

One of the state's top attractions is Dover Downs. The complex includes a hotel, a casino, and a harness racing track. It is also home to Dover International Speedway, where fans enjoy watching their favorite NASCAR drivers in action.

Delaware does not have any major sports teams, but it does have the Blue Rocks. The Blue Rocks are a Minor Leaue Baseball team in Wilmington. Many future Major League stars played for the team, including Carlos Beltran, Johnny Damon, and Jacoby Ellsbury.

Festivals, fairs, and other events also draw people to Delaware. The state has a number of museums and galleries where people can admire art and other unique treasures. Visitors also love shopping in Delaware's outlets and other retail shops. The state is one of the few that has no sales tax.

Tourism in Delaware brings in money for the state and provides jobs for state residents. The steady growth of tourism creates a wide variety of jobs in service industries, including restaurants, hotels, and motels.

Attracting Businesses

During the 1970s, many Delawareans were out of work. Business and government leaders came up with an unusual solution. Lawmakers changed the state's business laws to attract out-of-state companies, especially banks and credit card companies. Dozens of corporations took advantage of the laws and set up corporate offices in the Wilmington area. Delaware got a new nickname—"the Home of Corporations." These companies created new jobs and brought extra tax income to the state. At the same time, the need for offices and housing contributed to steady growth in the construction industry.

Today, thousands of banks and corporations have some connection to Delaware.

In 2008, the American economy took a major hit during the so-called Great Recession. Millions of Americans lost their jobs, and countless businesses folded. The people of Delaware suffered along with the rest of the country. By the beginning of 2010, more than thirty-eight thousand people were out of work. Wilmington was hit the hardest. Nearly 13 percent of workers in the city were unemployed. The state's last two auto manufacturing plants shut down. State employees were forced to take a pay cut. Governor Jack Markell praised the people of Delaware for remaining strong during the tough times. "I remain firmly convinced that our state's best days are ahead of us," he said.

A Changing Economy

Delaware—like the rest of the country—is facing some economic challenges. The manufacturing sector, a key part of the state's economy, is shrinking. The state's automobile plants never reopened after the Great Recession. However, the state is having success courting the aviation industry and gaining some jobs in that field. Local colleges and airports make it easy for aviation companies to work within the state—drawing more and more business to Delaware.

Aviation jobs are on the rise in Delaware.

Luckily, other sectors of the economy are growing to take the place of manufacturing. The financial industry is adding jobs year after year. In the future, this field, along with other industries that provide services rather than producing goods, is likely to increase and replace lost manufacturing jobs.

Delaware's state capitol building is called Legislative Hall.

5 Government

Delaware is a leader at both the state and national level. Delawareans like Joe Biden, who had a long career in the US Senate before serving as vice president, inspire political action across the nation. Biden's passionate defense of working-class families made him a leading voice on the national stage. Furthermore, Delaware's state government is a trailblazer on many important issues. For example, the 1971 Coastal Zone Act that protected the shores of Delaware was a forerunner of many other environmental protection laws across the United States.

Delaware's Constitution

The constitution of a state is its framework of government. Much like the US Constitution, it describes the duties of the state government's three branches: the executive, the legislative, and the judicial. The executive branch, headed by the governor, runs the affairs of the state. The legislature makes laws. The judicial branch is composed of courts that settle disputes or hear cases when laws are broken.

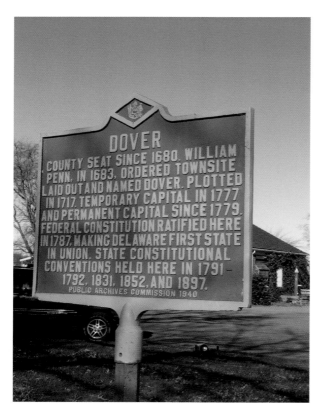

DOVER

COUNTY SEAT SINCE 1680. WILLIAM
PENN, IN 1683, ORDERED TOWNSITE
LAID OUT AND NAMED DOVER. PLOTTED
IN 1717. TEMPORARY CAPITAL IN 1777
AND PERMANENT CAPITAL SINCE 1779.
FEDERAL CONSTITUTION RATIFIED HERE
IN 1787, MAKING DELAWARE FIRST STATE
IN UNION. STATE CONSTITUTIONAL
CONVENTIONS HELD HERE IN 1791 –
1792, 1831, 1852, AND 1897.
PUBLIC ARCHIVES COMMISSION 1940

A marker in Dover commemorates the city's role in Delaware's political history.

During America's colonial period, the legislature in each colony could make its own laws, but the British monarch (the king or queen) could reject any law that he or she did not like. In 1776, when the Continental Congress approved the Declaration of Independence, the thirteen colonies became thirteen independent states and could write their own state constitutions. Delaware had a constitution ready by the end of 1776.

Over the next hundred-plus years, the legislature wrote three new constitutions. The state constitution in use today was written in 1897. However, Delawareans have added amendments, or made changes, to the constitution more than a hundred times. The process for amending the Delaware constitution is different from the process in any other state. The change must be approved by two-thirds of the legislature. The proposed amendment is then posted in newspapers in each county before the next election. After the election, the legislature votes again. If the proposal again wins two-thirds of the vote, the amendment is officially added to the constitution. The governor cannot veto, or reject, a constitutional amendment.

Separation of Powers

The three branches of government each have different sets of powers and responsibilities at both the state and federal level. The system is designed so that if one branch oversteps, another branch may check its overreach.

Woodburn is the governor's mansion in Delaware.

Executive Branch

The governor is the head of the state. He or she is responsible for approving or rejecting laws passed by the legislative branch. The governor prepares the state budget and suggests new laws. Along with the lieutenant governor, the attorney general, and the treasurer, the governor is elected to a four-year term. The governor can serve only two terms.

The Legislative Branch

The general assembly makes state laws. It is divided into two parts. The twenty-one senators are elected for four-year terms. The forty-one members of the house of representatives serve two-year terms. There is no limit on the number of terms a member of the general assembly can serve.

Senate chambers at the Legislative Hall

New Kent
County Courthouse

The Judicial Branch

All judges are appointed by the governor with the approval of the senate. These judges serve twelve-year terms. The highest court, the state supreme court, hears appeals from lower courts and can decide whether a law violates some part of the state constitution. Below the supreme court is the superior court, for criminal and civil cases. The **court of chancery** hears cases involving business disputes. The lowest courts hear cases involving matters such as family disputes or traffic offenses.

Passing a New Law

As in other states, before a law is passed in Delaware, it must go through an established process. Most laws begin with a suggestion or an idea from a Delaware resident or a member of the state legislature. The proposed law is called a bill.

The Delaware state legislature is called the Delaware General Assembly. Like the US Congress, it has a senate and a house of representatives. A bill may be introduced in either the senate or the house. From there, it is assigned to a committee. The committee members examine the bill. They hold hearings, or public meetings, to discuss the bill, and they may make changes to it. The committee can reject the bill and decide not to present it to the entire house. If the committee is satisfied with the bill, it is presented to the rest of the house.

The bill is read to the house three times. After the second reading, legislators can revise, or amend, the bill. They usually debate the bill after the third reading. After the third reading and the debates, the legislators vote on the bill. If the bill is approved, it is sent to the other house. There, it goes through a very similar process. If both houses agree on the bill, it is then sent to the governor. If the governor approves the bill, he or she can sign it into law. If the governor does not take any action, the bill will automatically become law after a certain amount of time. The governor can also veto, or reject, the bill. A vetoed bill can still become law if three-fifths of the members of both houses vote to override the governor's veto.

Local Government

The counties—New Castle, Kent, and Sussex—are the primary units for local government. The New Castle and Sussex governments consist of an elected council and council president. New Castle County also elects a county executive. Kent County uses an older system. It has an elected board of commissioners called the "levy court." The name comes from the old tradition of levying, or collecting, taxes.

The Ardens is a group of three villages that do not have an official government.

In addition, Delaware's large towns and cities generally elect a mayor and a council. A few hire a city manager rather than elect a mayor. Near the state's northern border, three villages known as the Ardens do not have any official government. Citizens work together to solve problems in the villages. The Ardens operate according to the ideas of Henry George, an author in the late 1800s. The townspeople own the land together rather than individually.

Staying Involved

The government is supposed to represent the people. Delawareans, like all Americans, are represented by both their state government and the federal government in Washington, DC. These two levels of government have different jobs, but they both act on behalf of their constituents—the people they represent. For this reason, it is important for Americans to stay involved in politics. If politicians do not know what their constituents want, they cannot act on their behalf.

Delaware.gov's websites can help you find your representatives.

Today, technology makes it easy to stay involved in politics. If you go to the website http://www.delaware.gov/topics/yourgovernment, you can find links to the web pages of your state and federal representatives, from senators to the state governor and attorney general. If you need to look up your local representative, you can go to http://www.legis.delaware.gov. Type your address into the box "Who Is My Legislator?" to find the members of the Delaware General Assembly who represent you.

These websites also provide you with the mailing addresses, email addresses, and phone numbers of your representatives. As always, talk to a trusted adult before contacting people. If you feel strongly about an issue, you can contact your representatives to make your opinion known. This is how representative government works. Always remember that being civil and polite makes people take your opinion more seriously.

Representing Delaware in Washington, DC

Like all states, Delaware is represented in the US Congress in Washington, DC. Each state elects two senators. Senators serve six-year terms, and they can be elected as many times as voters choose. Delaware's longest-serving senator was Joe Biden. He was first elected in 1972 at the age of twenty-nine. He served until January 2009, when he gave up his position to become vice president of the United States.

Delawareans elect one person to the US House of Representatives. A state's population determines its number of representatives. In 2018, Delaware was one of seven states that had only one representative. California has the most people and the most representatives of any state (fifty-three in 2018).

Joe Biden gives a speech in 2011.

Federal Supremacy

According to the US Constitution, federal law is supreme over state law. In case of a conflict, the federal law is followed, and state law is not. Courts can strike down state laws when they do not follow this rule. This is what occurred on August 2, 2016, when the Delaware Supreme Court ruled that the state's death penalty was unconstitutional. The court found that it violated the Sixth Amendment—concerning jury trials—because in Delaware it was left to the discretion of the judge, and not the jury, to choose when to apply the death penalty.

On May 9, 2017, the state legislature passed a new law that allowed the death penalty. According to the new law, juries would be responsible for deciding when to apply it. Judges, however, would have to approve. In this way, federal supremacy and the Constitution were respected by the Delaware legislature.

Glossary

abolitionist   A person who wanted to ban slavery in the lead-up to, and during, the Civil War.

blight   A disease, often one that affects plants.

climate change   The recent change in climate toward higher average temperatures and more frequent extreme weather events. It is due in part to human activity.

court of chancery   A kind of court that focuses on cases involving business disputes.

Kevlar   A very strong material developed and trademarked by DuPont in 1965 that is used to make bulletproof vests.

peninsula   A strip of land jutting out into an ocean or lake from the mainland.

Return Day   A tradition from colonial days that brings Delaware residents together in Georgetown to celebrate election results, including the winners and losers of the election.

smallpox   A viral disease that often involves a high fever and rash. Many Native Americans died from smallpox after Europeans arrived in North America.

truck farm   Farms, usually small, that produce vegetables and fruits that are transported by trucks to markets.

wampum   Beads made from seashells used in traditional Native American art and jewelry. Over time, wampum was used as money.

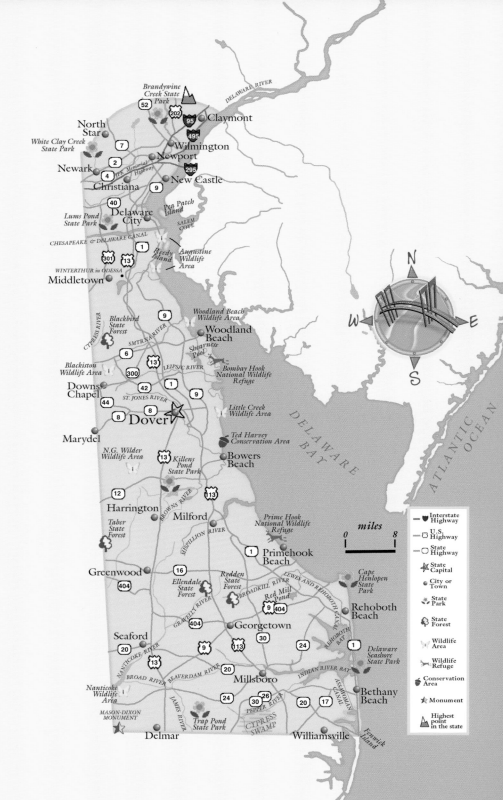

Delaware State Map and Map Skills

Questions

1. What state park is north of Claymont?

2. What beach is south of Rehoboth Beach?

3. Which US highway runs north-south?

4. To get from Greenwood to Prime Hook National Wildlife Refuge, which direction do you travel?

5. Which state park is west of Cypress Swamp?

6. Which town is south of Seaford?

7. What point of interest is north of Bowers Beach?

8. What monument is south of Nanticoke Wildlife Area?

9. What is the closest city or town south of Dover?

10. Which bay feeds into the Atlantic Ocean?

Answers

1. Brandywine Creek State Park
2. Bethany Beach
3. US-13
4. East
5. Trap Pond State Park
6. Delmar
7. Ted Harvey Conservation Area
8. Mason-Dixon Monument
9. Harrington
10. Delaware Bay

More Information

Books

Hossell, Karen. *Delaware, 1638–1776.* Voices from Colonial America. Washington, DC: National Geographic Society, 2006.

McManus, Lori. *Exploring the Delaware Colony.* North Mankato, MN: Capstone Press, 2016.

Stanley, Joseph. *Delaware (Lenape).* Spotlight on Native Americans. New York: PowerKids Press, 2016.

Websites

A Brief History of New Sweden in America
http://colonialswedes.net/History/History.html
The Swedish Colonial Society explains the circumstances surrounding New Sweden.

Delaware State Parks Passport Program
https://destateparks.com/Passport
Take selfies at all nineteen "passport photo" locations in Delaware State Parks to win prizes.

Kid-Friendly Events in Delaware
https://www.visitdelaware.com/things-to-do/events-festivals/kids-family
Delaware's official tourism website provides a list of fun events for kids and their families.

The Lenni-Lenape Indians
http://www2.mtlaurelschools.org/MLHistory/lennilenape.htm
Mount Laurel Township school district presents interesting facts about the Native American tribe that inhabited parts of Delaware and New Jersey.